look at us

SHAKE

the sky

look at us shake the sky

SAINT KNIVES

to whom it concerns,
you mean the world to me

table of contents

chapter 1:
love

chapter 2:
loss

acknowledgement

so many people have inadvertently played a massive role in inspiring this work, either with words, actions, or feelings.

a few amazing authors i personally know who have released very important work:

venus di'kahdijah selenite, carmen brady, leylâ çolpan, daphne calhoun, june gehringer, casey plett, and many others.

other authors who have greatly influenced this work, dead or alive, include:

rupi kaur, virginia woolf, sylvia plath, and walt whitman.

also the amazingly talented

ashley fly

(who can be found on twitter: @locustbones) provided the photography for the front and back cover.

thank you.

preface

"most of this book came to me in my dreams,"

...in particular whispers that sunk into
parts of my brain like hooks,
unwilling to let go even after i awoke.
the thing about trauma is that it is not
just a singular event: it lives with you.
it breathes your air. it's always there
and it tends to not
remind you of its presence until the
worst possible moment.

"my traumas, which began
when I was still a child..."

and continued throughout my life,
have snowballed
into an immovable force
that colours every single action i take
in life. as one would surmise,
this also means that
everything i write has a traumatic
history behind it.

"so much happened to me in the year 2017"

i moved away from chicago,
which was simultaneously my
sanctuary and my purgatory, and
settled in omaha.
i began extreme social
isolation and really buckled down on
my writing. i released "la mer" in april
and "i wish i was dead," in august.
i had written a chapbook in 2015, but

*"releasing these two books made me feel like a
real artist for the first time in my life."*

"look at us shake the sky,"
i feel, is a natural continuation of
those two books, while also being
something different entirely.
my isolation, examination of
past trauma from living in chicago,
and new trauma from living in omaha,
all went into something that i believe is
my most personal work yet.
i am truly proud of this book,
and i hope it can help even just a
single person who is struggling.

you are loved.

chapter 1

love

"meeting you"

the medic is better acquainted

with the rhythm of your heart

than I could ever claim to be

my teeth ached

with a feeling unnatural

the gap between them

always burdened my thoughts

you are not as alone

as once thought

"speak up"

i long for a kiss

that no one can see

and an unburdened view

of an american heart

if i can't call out your name

in the middle of the night

what hope is left?

a sour girl, lost to the world

a relief to beggars in bandages

it is in lust

where your words are the

loudest

"oasis"

i wish you would come over here

to explain things

my body is a desert

a lonely expanse that's never properly

before been charted

"help"

tell me

what i have done to you

my hands are without grace

but could still heal

"a good defense"

there is safety, they say

in numbers

even if that number

is just one

you are your own most capable

protector

"passion"

of course

i want to be with you

it's with you that i feel

soft

delicate

valued

appreciated

warm

whole

"a blessing"

loving you

was the scariest thing i could have
done

i am so glad i found bravery

"to wish impossible things"

tell me

am i selfish

to want you wholly and completely

to be my entire world?

"a message"

you matter

"request"

i hope you can

find some sort of use

for this heart

i gave you

"missed connections"

searching for:

someone to love

my brown skin

in ways I can't

just yet

"tinder"

i want to

kiss

every single girl

with a septum piercing

you already have my heart

"changing"

my body

is made of autumnal flowers

and so many whispers

"personality disorder"

i have imagined our life together

before you've even paid for the check

i am so sorry

"a time to be so cared for"

the warmth in your cheeks

when I hold your facc in my hands

is a feeling I have been chasing

for years

"hands away"

there is too much

that I want desperately in this world

but what I need

is strength

to have my words blot out the sun

"shiver"

fall in love

with someone whose fingers

feel like poetry on your skin

"to fathers"

your daughters

will look up at you

and see the sun

"the thousandth date"

if nothing else

we can share the same air

as a way to pass the time

"courting"

she brought the entirety of her soul

and her heart

and her guts

expecting a fair trade

"waiting"

she tried one million different ways

to love herself

as practice for him

"me too"

i survived.

"the stars"

i found out you were a cancer

my pisces heart sang in triumph

i want to get my hopes up

this time

"my people"

even when i am alone

i never truly fccl alone

knowing that all over the world exists
my tribe

loving

learning

laughing

living

breathing

in unison

we have so much to celebrate

"progress"

i think i am in love with more than just

the idea of you

"heart, mind, and ears"

here

here

and here

"untitled"

I want love

that will make me forget

all of the times I said I hate love

"divine"

i fell in love with you and i haven't even met you yet

i spend all of my time, free or not, daydreaming of what i'll
say to you at the airport

marveling at how much taller I am

smelling your hair as if the secret of life is your aroma

i think of the way you'll kiss me, like you starve for the
honey on my lips

i envision the way you touch my arms will be soft and
delicate, still shooting electricity

through my veins

i consider the way you'll look at me when i've undressed for
you, when i'm bearing all

of my shame and self doubts inches away from you

and how your touch will go from gentle to rough when i ask

your fingers gracing my nipples like you're lazily pointing to
the sky and connect

constellations

i hope you'll forgive me

this is a body not used to love

i fell in love with someone who i think will still want to kiss
me after i show them what i

hate most about myself

chapter 2

loss

"untitled"

shc was born from a mound of ashes

and a dream of losses undisturbed

was sleeping on the beach such a good

idea amongst such turmoil?

life itself has become a harrowing
pursuit

for the privilege of knowing g-d

or just a resistance to storms

"chateau"

and i know the sun will rise again

even without tight fisted prayers

from those who cherish me

i have the face of a young daughter

lips, eyes, cheeks

a jaw that overexerts itself

without breaking too many promises,

I think that I will be okay

a survivor of art at the mercy of lovers

"spiral"

my body and soul

has been filled with nothing but

violence

for years

it is so hard to know anything more

than that

"super natural"

the only ghost

that haunts this cold house of ours

is the spectre of our former love

it feels almost

familiar

when it briefly passes through us

and then leaves without a trace

"dark days"

it is revolutionary to me

and reactionary to you

to cut off all my hair

just to make you kiss your teeth

and lament

that you no longer find me pretty

"untitled"

i am more than

what my rapist took from me

"the night we met"

you kissed my open palms

expecting to taste honey

you have only known disappointment

since we met

"the high road"

i have dreamt of ways to keep you

i could bind your wrists with promises

the likes of which pour from my mouth

and taste like vinegar

but i know i must let go

"here comes the feeling"

tonight, i am going to dream

a woman is going to appear,

haggard and

broken down

she will tell me how everything i taste

will

turn to dirt in my mouth

and everything i touch

will slide through

desperate fingers

the next day, you'll leave me

"honest mistake"

you could leave me

a thousand times

i would still ask you

to stay

"untitled"

let me go

before you have a chance

to leave me first

"first weeks"

do you break the hearts

of all the girls you spend time with

or am i special in that regard?

"our love's funeral"

i grieve you

pine for you

and eulogize you

while you still sleep beside me

"untitled"

the emptiness inside of me is insatiable

"gemini"

i paid attention to the way you left me

i studied your motions

i focused on your speech

especially the lack of questions

and the evenness of your tone

your bag was packed

like you had packed

days ago for a routine trip

you had done this

so often to other girls

that i had to be another dress rehearsal

"echo"

you will never

kiss me

again

my lips are trying to adjust

"untitled"

you are a story

i wish i could never know the ending of

"bullet proof"

tonight is the first night

in my entire life

where sleeping alone

feels like a promise

not a threat

"disarm"

i just want autonomy   .

and good feelings

wounds that stand a chance of healing

and the skill to find my way home

,

.

"acceptance"

'couldn't you just be a boy!'

she cried

as if she had a shortage

of suns

"commands"

while i still live, take my breath

while i still write, take my words

oh, while i still think, take my thoughts

it's as slave

not ruler

that i offer the extent of my riches

who are you without my gifts?

"we became dark"

my skin carries so many secrets

it's known the wandering touch

of singers

and poets

and workers whose rough hands

fashioned steel

history leaps out of my pores

like an offering

"welcome home"

come in. take your jacket off.

breathe.

how was your journey?

how was your time away from me?

pleasing?

"you swore

it would be different this time"

don't you love me back?

i have tasted my own grief

over and over

it tastes more like blood

than i remember

and i can smell

the perfume of the shiksa

you told me not to worry about

"untitled"

my closed mouth

is where my desires pass away

"bodies"

i am so ugly in an intimate way

the rolls of my stomach spill out from

under my shirt

defiant, always wanting to be seen

stubborn hair clings to my leg

it's avoided my blades

five or six times now

my chin juts out with pride

i am not to be loved

and yet

the faint edges of love

comes to me in dreams

"purpose"

even if it

kills

me

i will deliver my soul to absolution

"living with bpd"

your desire for love

does not make you a monster

you deserve beauty

"to dahlia"

you have survived so many things

built solely to destroy you

"untitled"

i have been in mourning since we met

"(an ode to

'i sing the body electric'

by walt whitman)"

i scream the body electric

while I learn that blood runs on the

outside of my skin

just as quickly as it does

internally

my misery does not belong solely to me

and could never

by any meaningful stretch

of the imagination

it belongs to you

and I

and every person on this planet

people tied together

by the worst that the world has to offer

i should leave home

and never again return

unless the west spits me back out again

Saint Knives is a Chicago-based poet, author, speaker, and musician whose past literary accomplishments include debuting at number one for LGBT poetry on Amazon in 2017.

Made in the USA
Middletown, DE
31 August 2020